D1540989

BUSY LITTLE

ARTIST

SALLY HEWITT

ILLUSTRATED BY
PENNY DANN

JellyBean Press
New York

This book belongs to

Design: Alison Fenton
Design assistants: Karen Fenton
and Caroline Johnson
Editor: Sue Hook
Photography: Mike Galletly

The author and publishers would like to thank
Val Abercrombie and the children who made the projects
to be photographed: Harriet Bates, Elizabeth de Gatacre,
Alice Jarvis, Claire Linnette, Madeleine O'Shea,
Rebecca Rand, Jemma Rowe, Camilla Sutton

First published in 1990 by
Conran Octopus Limited
37 Shelton Street, London WC2H 9HN

© text 1990 Conran Octopus Limited
© illustration 1990 Penny Dann

This 1990 edition published by
JellyBean Press,
distributed by Outlet Book Company, Inc.,
a Random House Company,
225 Park Avenue South, New York, New York 10003

Printed and bound in Great Britain

ISBN 0-517-036045

87654321

Contents

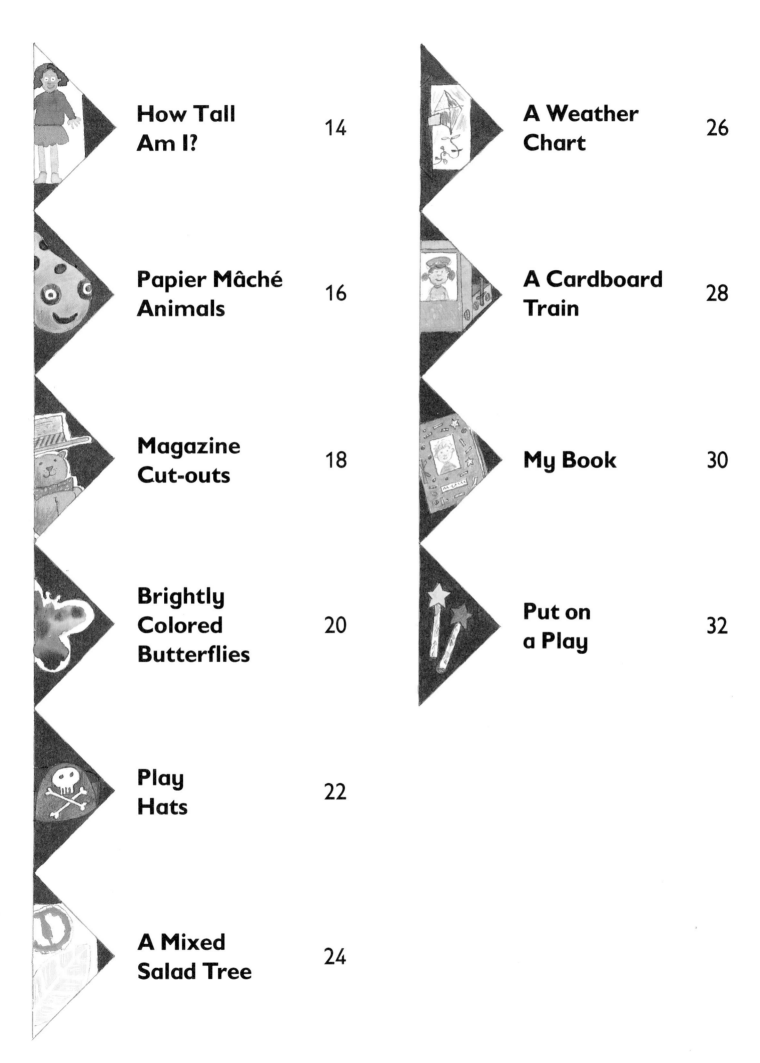

How to be an Artist

Do you like cutting and pasting, drawing and painting, tearing and folding and making interesting things? Basic craft supplies, odds and ends, busy hands and lots of ideas are all you need to be an artist. Ask an adult to help you whenever you see this symbol ★.

▶ **Find out how you can be an artist**

Get a box for your tools. Put a pencil, crayons, safety scissors, paint and glue brushes, cellophane tape, empty yogurt cups, glue and some paints into your box.

What would you like to make? A present for a friend, a decoration for your room, a robot or a puppet? Now you're ready with tools, materials and your ideas.

You will need a bigger box for your materials. Collect lots of interesting things: different kinds of paper, buttons, beads, shells, empty boxes, cardboard tubes, cotton, pretty pieces of fabric, magazines and cards. What else can you think of?

Are you ready to be an artist?

Take care!

Keep tiny items – such as buttons or beads – away from small children.

Pins and Badges

Make a badge of your own age or initial and decorate it yourself.

I'm drawing 4 because I'm 4 years old.

Do you like my S for Sam?

1 Draw the first letter of your name or the number of your age on a piece of cardboard. You can draw round a plastic letter or number if you have one.

You will need

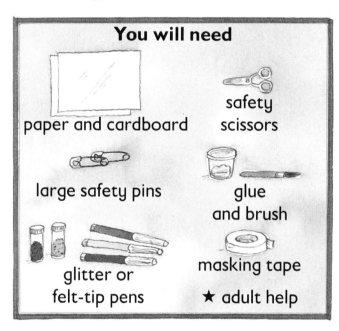

paper and cardboard

safety scissors

large safety pins

glue and brush

glitter or felt-tip pens

masking tape

★ adult help

I'm coloring mine striped with felt-tip pens.

I'll shake the loose glitter onto some paper to save it.

2 Cut out the letter or number and decorate it. You can paint it with glue and sprinkle on glitter or color it in.

Birthday presents

Make birthday presents for your friends. Make a badge of their initials or age. You can pin the badge to a birthday card you have made for them.

Mine's ready!

Let's ask Mommy to stick the pins on our badges.

3 ★ Stick the safety pin to the back of the badge with a piece of masking tape. Press the tape down firmly.

A Model Robot

Don't throw away empty boxes, packages or cardboard tubes. Use them to make a model. You can even make it move!

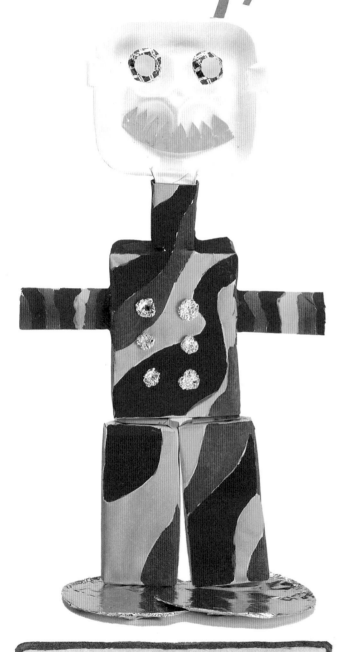

You will need

a collection of boxes, cardboard tubes and decorating materials

safety scissors

masking tape

shelf paper

glue and brush

paints, water and brushes

Some more ideas

Try making a boat that floats. Don't paint it! Make a truck with wheels that go round, a space ship or a totem pole decorated with feathers.

Cardboard tubes are good for arms.

I'll use this big box for the body.

1 Place your boxes and tubes out on the table in the shape you want for your model robot.

2 Wrap the boxes up in shelf paper, like a package, so that they are easier to paint. Use masking tape to stick the paper in place over the boxes.

4 You can cut out rectangles of cardboard and bend them in the middle to make a moving joint. Use masking tape to attach one side of the joint to the leg and one side to the body.

3 Glue the boxes firmly together. Snip round the end of the cardboard tubes to make flaps. Press the flaps out to make a flat surface for covering with thick glue. Glue the cardboard tubes in place.

5 Decorate your robot with milk or soda bottle tops, aluminium foil and cardboard to make eyes, knobs and antennae. Paint it brightly with several colors. What are you going to call it?

Paper Bag Puppets

Use paper bags to make puppets, and put on a show for your friends.

You will need

paper bags

colored paper

crumpled newspaper

safety scissors

rubber bands

masking tape

cardboard (paper towel) tubes

glue and brush

yarn or cotton

★ adult help

This is going to be a pig.

These pointed ears look like a fox.

1 ★ Make ears by twisting rubber bands just below the top 2 corners of the paper bag. Make sure you don't tear the bag.

2 ▶ Stuff crumpled newspaper inside the bag. You can put an extra piece in where you want the nose to be.

4 ▶ Decorate the head with glued colored paper to make the face. Cut yarn whiskers and attach with masking tape.

3 ▶ Push a cardboard tube up into the newspaper and pull the bottom of the bag down over the tube. ★ Twist a rubber band round the bag and the tube to hold them firmly together.

Put on a puppet show

When you have made several puppets, make up a story about them. Hide behind the back of a chair and hold the puppets over the top. You can act out your story for your friends.

9

A Portrait Gallery

A portrait is a picture that looks like someone. Draw a picture of your friend.

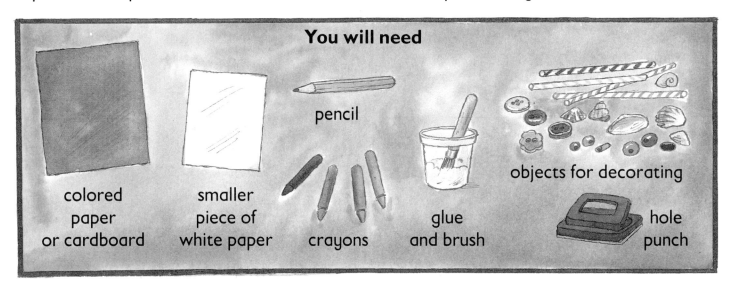

You will need

pencil

objects for decorating

colored paper or cardboard

smaller piece of white paper

crayons

glue and brush

hole punch

1 ▶ Look carefully at your friend's face before you start your picture.

2 ▶ Draw the shape of the face on the white paper. Use a pencil.

▶ **3** Draw the face and hair using the right colors.

▶ **4** Turn the paper over. Put small dabs of glue on the corners and middle. Glue your portrait on to the colored cardboard, leaving a border around the edge of the portrait.

▶ **5** Punch 2 holes in the top edge of the frame. Glue shells, buttons, beads or cut-up drinking straws around it.

Hang your portrait

Thread yarn or ribbon through the holes in the frame. Name your portrait and hang it on the wall.

Collage Pictures

Collect different materials and use them to make a collage picture for your wall.

Here are some ideas for your collection:

1 Feel the different textures of the things you have collected. What picture can you use them for?

You will need

construction paper and cardboard

collected materials

glue and brush

safety scissors

2 If you are using sand or glitter, spread glue on to your thick paper and sprinkle the sand or glitter on to the glue.

3 Cut pieces of paper or material into the shapes you want. Glue the backs and then glue them on to your paper.

My frame is wider all around than my picture.

Can I use some of your shells to decorate mine?

4 When you have finished, frame your picture and hang it with your portrait.

Some more ideas for collage pictures

Make a snow scene with cotton, glitter and paper doilies.

Make a textured pattern using things that feel different.

Make an underwater picture with blue and green tissue-paper sea and candy wrapper fish.

How Tall Am I?

Make a chart for your bedroom to see how tall you are. Keep a record of your height.

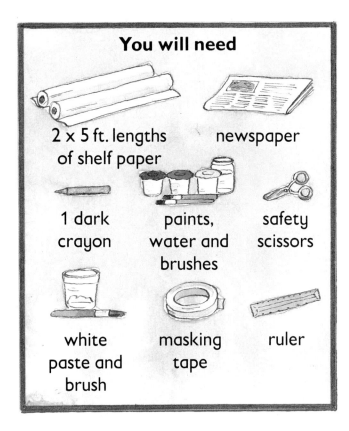

You will need

2 x 5 ft. lengths of shelf paper

newspaper

1 dark crayon

paints, water and brushes

safety scissors

white paste and brush

masking tape

ruler

2 Take your shoes off. Lie down on the paper with your hands by your sides and your feet out sideways. Get your friend to draw round you with a dark crayon.

1 Cut 2 x 5 ft. lengths of shelf paper. Lay one sheet on the kitchen floor. Attach each corner with a piece of masking tape.

3 Spread newspaper over the floor under your drawing. Paint in the figure so that it looks just like you.

Cut and color the shape of your hand-span. Glue the shapes up the side of the chart. How many hands high are you?

4 When the painting is dry, cut around it carefully and put it paint side down on the newspaper. Brush white paste all over the back and then glue it on to your second length of paper.

How Tall Am I ?

5 Write HOW TALL AM I? at the top and attach the chart to the wall so the bottom touches the floor. Mark equally spaced measurements up one side.

Papier Mâché Animals

Papier mâché objects are strong and easy to make. Try making some animals using balloons as molds.

You will need

bowl

flour and water paste and brush

safety scissors

sheets of newspaper

blown-up balloon tied with string

paints, water and brushes

This one looks like a caterpillar.

I like this big fat one.

1 Spread newspaper on the table. Tear some more newspaper into strips. Mix 1 part flour and 3 parts water until smooth and creamy. Choose a balloon. What kind of animal could you make it into?

2 ▶ Brush the flour and water paste on to the newspaper strips and cover the balloon evenly with them. Repeat this until there are about 3 layers of newspaper pasted on to the balloon.

4 ▶ When it is quite dry, it will feel hard when you tap it. Use paints to color it brightly all over. Don't forget to wash your brush before you use a new color.

3 ▶ Hang the balloon up to dry somewhere cool and airy. It will take at least a day before it is ready to paint.

5 ▶ When the paint is dry, pop the balloon by cutting off the end with the string tied to it. You could decorate your animal with eyes, a mouth or a tail.

Decoration ideas

Plume, fin or tail
Cut this shape from cardboard. Fold the flaps, one backward, one forward. Glue them down on to your animal.

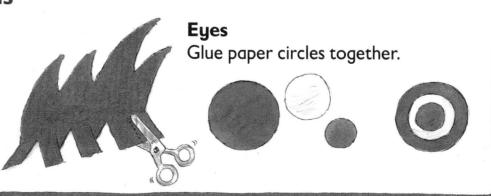

Eyes
Glue paper circles together.

Magazine Cut-outs

Cut out pictures from old magazines and catalogues and use them to make a new picture of your own.

You will need

old magazines and catalogues

white paste or glue and brush

safety scissors

hole punch

plain paper

ribbon

1 ▶ Choose pictures of people, children, animals or toys and cut them out. Sort the pictures into sets.

2 ▶ Arrange the cut-outs on the plain paper. Glue them down with white paste or glue when you have decided where you want them to go.

3 ▶ Cut out a hat, a head, a body, legs and feet from 5 different people. Mix them up and put them together again to make a funny figure.

Collecting pictures

Put your sets of pictures into envelopes and mark the front TOYS, CHILDREN, ANIMALS or PEOPLE. Use them for making cards, or decorating your pictures or play hats.

4 ▶ Make a book of funny figures. Punch holes in the side of the pictures and tie them together with ribbon. Give all the figures silly names like Molly Mixture and Wobbly Wilbur.

Brightly Colored Butterflies

Brighten up your room with a display of colorful butterflies.

You will need

white paper and pencil

glue and brush

white paper glue and brush

safety scissors

cup cake pan

newspaper

brightly colored paints, water and brushes

1 ▶ Spread some newspaper. Mix red, yellow and blue paints with a little white paper glue to thicken them. Keep the colors apart so they don't run into each other.

2 ▶ Cut rectangles of white paper into different sizes to make big, middle-sized and small butterflies. Fold them in half.

3 Start at the folded center and draw half of the body and one side of a butterfly's wings on the paper. Now cut out the butterfly shape and open it out.

4 Paint a pattern on 1 side of the butterfly. Fold it in half and press the 2 sides together to print the pattern on to both wings. Now open the wings.

5 Try choosing just 2 of the primary colors, (red, blue and yellow,) to make your pattern. What happens when you press the wings together and the colors mix? You have a new color!

Brighten up your room

Use up your mixed paints by painting flowers on a large piece of paper. Glue on some small butterflies, leaving the wings free.

Glue a large butterfly on to the window where it will catch the light.

Play Hats

Make a collection of hats for dressing-up. They are lots of fun and easy to make.

You will need

- colored cardboard and paper
- masking tape
- pencil
- felt-tip pens
- ruler
- cotton
- safety scissors
- milk or soda bottle tops
- glue and brush
- sparkly beads and sequins

Animal hats

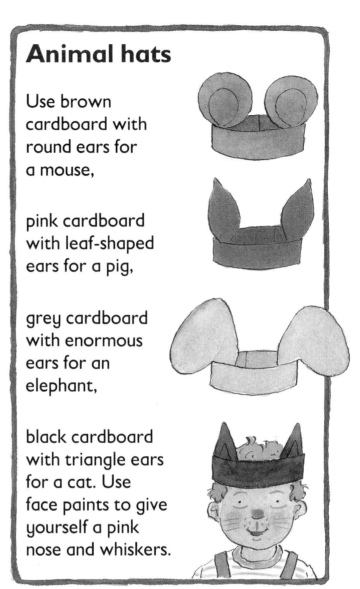

Use brown cardboard with round ears for a mouse,

pink cardboard with leaf-shaped ears for a pig,

grey cardboard with enormous ears for an elephant,

black cardboard with triangle ears for a cat. Use face paints to give yourself a pink nose and whiskers.

1 ▶ To make a hat band, cut a strip of cardboard about 2½ ins. wide, and long enough to go around your head. Use different colored cardboard for each hat you make.

3 ▶ Draw a skull and cross-bones on white cardboard. Give it black eyes and teeth. Cut out and stick on to half a circle of black cardboard. Glue the black cardboard on to a black hat band.

2 ▶ Measure the strip of cardboard around your head. Overlap the 2 ends and glue them together with masking tape to make a circle which fits comfortably.

4 ▶ Cut zig-zag shapes from a wider hat band to make a crown. Glue on cotton and sparkly beads and sequins to look like jewels.

A Mixed Salad Tree

Keep old or dried out fruit and vegetables to print an exotic tree for a wall hanging.

You will need

leaves

fruit and vegetables, including a cabbage

blunt-tipped knife

safety scissors

paints, water and brushes

plastic paint trays or plates

white paper glue and brush

chopping board

shelf paper

masking tape

newspaper
★ adult help

This long piece is for the tree.

So this one must be for the leaf, fruit and vegetable prints.

1 Lay plenty of newspaper out on the floor. Roll out and cut 1 long and 1 shorter piece of shelf paper over the newspaper. Stick the ends down firmly with tape.

2 Mix brown and some brightly colored paints with some white paper glue to thicken them. Pour the paint into plastic trays or plates.

4 Dip a piece of cabbage into the brown paint, then press it down on to the large sheet of paper to make a print. Print it over and over again to make the trunk and branches of a tree.

3 ★ With adult help cut the fruit and vegetables in half. Hold each one steady with one hand and cut well away from your fingers. Cut as straight as you can. Cut a small cabbage into quarters.

5 Paint the leaves bright colors, then press them paint side down on to the smaller piece of paper. Dip the fruit and vegetable halves in the paint and print them too. Cut them out and stick them on to your tree.

More decorations

Make some brightly colored birds using collage and some butterflies to put on the tree.

A Weather Chart

What's the weather like today? Open the windows of your weather chart to record the weather.

You will need

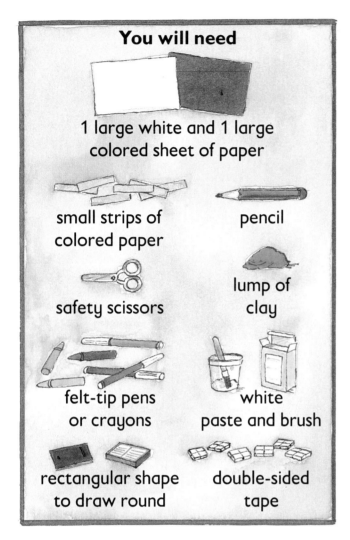

1 large white and 1 large colored sheet of paper

small strips of colored paper

pencil

safety scissors

lump of clay

felt-tip pens or crayons

white paste and brush

rectangular shape to draw round

double-sided tape

1 Find a rectangular shape like a small notebook or a cassette box. Draw around it 6 times on the colored paper, leaving a space between each shape, to make 6 windows.

This week's weather

Make a chart to record what sort of weather we are having this week.

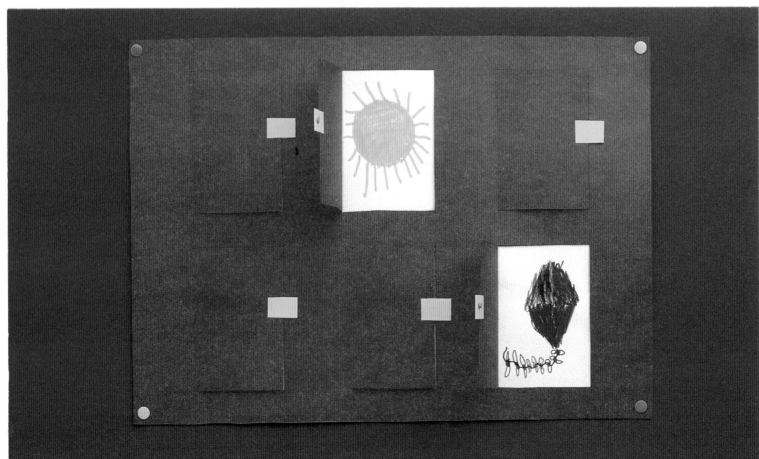

2 Stick a little piece of clay under the pencil outline of a window. Push your scissors through the paper into the clay underneath.

3 Cut and fold open all the windows. Put the colored paper on top of the white paper and draw around the inside of the windows to make matching rectangular shapes on the white paper.

4 Draw different weather pictures in each rectangle. Open the windows. Glue the colored paper on to the white.

5 Label the windows to match your weather pictures. Cut 6 small strips of colored paper. Fold each one in half and glue to the edge of each window to make a handle. Write "What's the weather like today?" across the top of the chart.

A Cardboard Train

Save some big cardboard boxes to make a train with cars and a signal box.

Take your favorite toys for a ride.

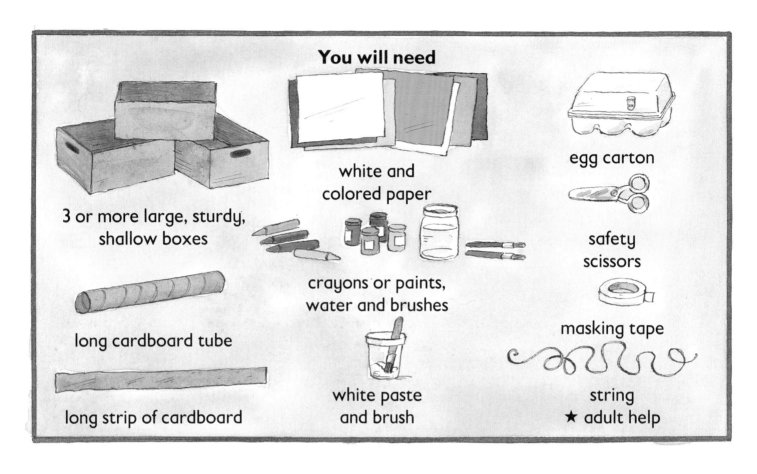

You will need

3 or more large, sturdy, shallow boxes

long cardboard tube

long strip of cardboard

white and colored paper

crayons or paints, water and brushes

white paste and brush

egg carton

safety scissors

masking tape

string
★ adult help

1. Take 2 boxes. Hold one upright and the other flat. Push the flat one inside the upright one to make an L shape. Tape the sides together.

2. Draw the view that the engine driver sees from his cabin and glue it on the inside of the upright box. Draw a picture of yourself driving the train and glue it on the outside.

3. To make a lever, hold the cardboard tube upright against the side of the box and put the cardboard strip over it. Attach the strip with masking tape. Glue STOP and GO labels beside it. Cut and paint wheels and buffers and glue them in place.

4. Glue colored paper knobs on to the bottom of an egg carton to make a control panel. Use tape to attach it underneath the window in the cabin.

5. Use more boxes for the cars. ★ Attach them to the train with string threaded through each box and knotted. Put your passengers on board.

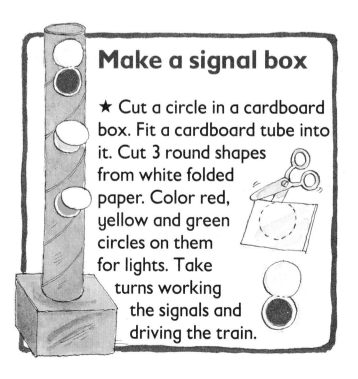

Make a signal box

★ Cut a circle in a cardboard box. Fit a cardboard tube into it. Cut 3 round shapes from white folded paper. Color red, yellow and green circles on them for lights. Take turns working the signals and driving the train.

My Book

A book of your own is fun to make. You can put whatever you choose in it.

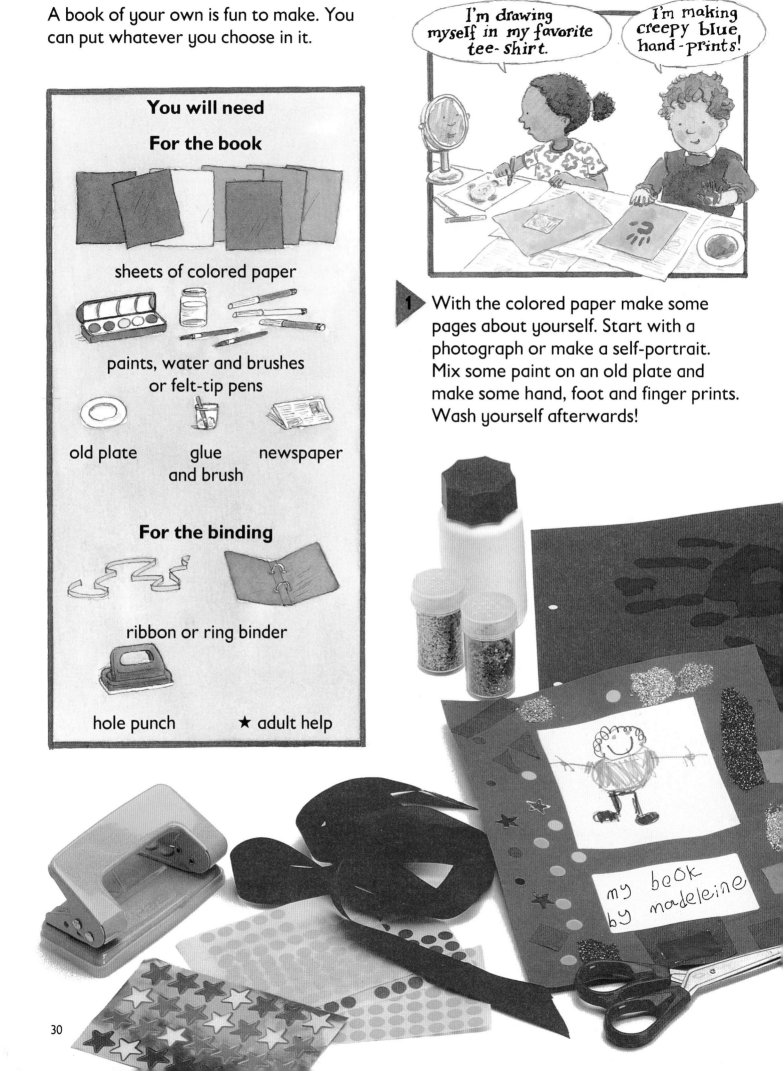

I'm drawing myself in my favorite tee-shirt.

I'm making creepy blue hand-prints!

You will need

For the book

sheets of colored paper

paints, water and brushes
or felt-tip pens

old plate

glue
and brush

newspaper

For the binding

ribbon or ring binder

hole punch   ★ adult help

1 ▶ With the colored paper make some pages about yourself. Start with a photograph or make a self-portrait. Mix some paint on an old plate and make some hand, foot and finger prints. Wash yourself afterwards!

my book
by madeleine

2 ▶ Write your height, weight and birthday. Draw your favorite food, toys and television programs. Glue in pictures of your family and friends.

3 ▶ When your book is ready punch 2 holes in each page and tie them with ribbon.
★ Or you could clip the pages into a ring binder. Glue a photograph on the front and write MY BOOK by: write in your own name.

Collecting souvenirs

When you go on vacation or on an outing, look out for small souvenirs. Keep brochures, menus, postcards, paper napkins or badges to put in your book.

Put on a Play

You can use some of the things you have learned to make to put on a play with your friends.

Here are some ideas

▶ Make characters so that each of you can play a part.

Use your Play Hats (page 22).

Make a witch's hat from black paper.

Add a big star to a blue hat band to make a fairy's hat.

Make a wand from a thin roll of newspaper wrapped in aluminium foil. Add a black star for a wicked wizard or a yellow star for a good fairy.

▶ Try on some masks made from paper plates and cardboard tubes. Make holes for eyes.

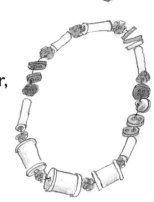

▶ You can make garlands and necklaces from crumpled tissue paper, empty thread spools, bright colored buttons and pasta. Thread them all on to thin string.

▶ Now decide where you want your play to be set. It might be in a forest, on a farm, in a fairy castle, on a desert island or in a snowy country.

▶ Make up a story and act it for an audience. Try a Christmas Play, a Chanukah Play or a Birthday Play.

Have fun!